Mistaking the Nature of the Posthuman

Steve Sneyd

For Ken Faig
Best Wishes
Steve Sn.

Hilltop Press

British Library Cataloguing in Publication Data
A Catalogue record for this book is available from the
British Library

ISBN 978-0-905262-42-0

HILLTOP PRESS
4 Nowell Place, Almondbury,
Huddersfield, HD5 8PB.

Hilltop Press titles are distributed overseas by BBR/NSFA
www.bbr-online.com/catalogue

Printed in Scotland by Oakleaf Design & Print, New Galloway, DG7 3RX. Tel: 0845 867 8983

INTRODUCTION

Those gnomic sardonicisms we've all encountered, of the "You don't have to be mad to work here, but it helps" type, combine for their displayers an enigmatic kind of comfort, if only of the circumstance-enduring sort, with an assertion of individuality somehow preserved intact, paradoxically, via all-purpose, generations-sanctioned recognition of shared universal principles of stoic humour as an abiding life force.

Recently, to get nearer the point, I saw wall-mounted, in a pub that seemed, remarkably, to survive in a timewarp, having the nature of a local from decades back - to be precise, the Falcon at Littleborough, Lancs - just such a pokerwork-mottoish piece of folk wisdom, but one completely new to me. It read "Build A System That Only A Fool Can Use & Only A Fool Will Use It."

Given the tsunami of changes in recent years, and how little the Future-as-was that is our now Now resembles as a whole or in detail the predictions of even a few years back, then it might seem that only a fool would consider attempting to use that most unforgiving-of-error of systems for manipulating experience-cum-memory-cum-imagination into patterned words, ie poetry, to attempt snatching snapshots out of near, middle or far futures, thereby to as it were happy slap our descendants - optimistically assuming they survive imminent disaster swarms, of course - and indeed other intelligent entities, record the responses, and from those encounters bring back, minced and crushed - and, as the form of many of those poems here implies,dragging the records of such across, through or over, the time barrier, readily, indeed probably inescapably, involves sacrifice of much data redundancy, an enforced compression to core informational essentials - a record of those sightings, as far as is impossibly possible free of false significance, though doubtless not of the misinterpretations grown of the inevitably vast sociocultural differences between those lives further up the timeslope and us down it here, even if they and we share the necessity of confronting the madness of the incomprehensibly vast, indifferent universe with madnesses of individualised response.

Still, the challenge to try is one that this fool, myself, has long been unable to resist.*

So, without any more ado of introductory verbal extrusion, you are now welcomingly invited to enter this fool's timeship; step through the portal, and you'll find a selection of pieces, previously published since the start of the 21st century but never previously collected together. Explore, enjoy.

* NOTE: In saying this in the first person, I hope no one will suspect me of being foolish enough to attempt to claim that I am in the least unique in this foolishness; for a very long time (just how long is a matter for MUCH discussion - Chaucer's

House of Fame with its space satellites and matter transmission, anyone?), there have been poets who, as Shelley** put it, try to serve as "the mirrors of the gigantic shadows which futurity casts upon the present". Today, a remarkable number, occasionally or often, move out of the comfort - or discomfort - zone of the continuous present to attempt to capture envisioned futures and mind-grapple with their inhabitants, as even a cursory exploration into the field of what can be called science fiction or, on occasion, fuzzy as the term's meaning by now is, speculative poetry, will discover.

** In his 'In Defense of Poetry'

ABOUT THE AUTHOR :

Described by Ian McMillan as "the best science-fiction poet in the land"+, Steve Sneyd's poetry, in this genre, also dark fantasy, Arthurian, "mainstream" etc, has appeared in well over a thousand magazines, anthologies etc, in many countries, on the Net, and been heard on various radio stations (including BBC R4's Stanza in Space special) and Yorkshire TV. He has read at many venues, including various festivals, SF conventions, and two planetaria. His many published articles include numerous on aspects of science fiction poetry and its history, and books on the field, two of them subsequently archived on the Net. Since 1991 he has edited the genre poetry newsletter Data Dump. He has been a member of the Science Fiction Poetry Association since its foundation.

+Yorkshire Post, April 6, 2007

OTHER POETRY COLLECTIONS by **STEVE SNEYD :** (only those known to be still in print : can be ordered from BBR website.)

AHASUERUS ON MARS (Atlantean Publications) - long SF narrative poem;
AT THE THIRTEENTH HOUR, 2nd edn, Night Visions Press, USA - dark fantasy;
BAD NEWS FROM THE STARS, Ocean View Books, USA (in Ace Double format with Bruce Boston flash fictions) - science fiction;
THE PENNINE TRIANGLE, Othername Press - SF (with J.C. Hartley & John F. Haines);
SPIDERGRAMS, Dark Diamonds Press - SF/DF mindmap poems, with Andy Cocker art;
THREE STAR CHAMBER, Krax Rump Press - SF/DF haikuform in palmtop format;
WHAT TIME HAS USE FOR, 3rd edn, K.T.Publications - Arthurian poems; also (few left)
THE POET'S VOICE #1, New Series - Steve Sneyd Retrospective, selected by Fred Beake.

ACKNOWLEDGEMENTS

These poems previously appeared in the following magazines and anthologies:

UK.: Alt.Hist; Angel Body/BBR 24; Awen; Bard; Breathe; Chanticleer; Chimera; Eastern Rainbow; Focus; Future Dreaming; Gentle Reader; Handshake; Inclement; Inner Mysteries; Is Poetry Really A Green Energy Source?; Jupiter; Konfluence; Monomyth Supplement; Moodswing; Neon Highway; Old Rossum's Book of Practical Robots; Omega; Parameter; Premonitions; Purple Patch; Quarry; Raven; Roadworks; The Sun Doesn't Always Shine; 10th Muse. CANADA: On Spec. FRANCE: Paris-Atlantic. GERMANY: Litspeak. USA: Dreams and Nightmares; Fairy Tale Graveyard; Fantasy Commentator; Hadrosaur Tales; Illumen; Minotaur; Opossum Holler Tarot; Pablo Lennis; Poetry At Lehani's; Skug; Snow Birds In Cloud Hands; Snow Monkey; Star*Line; Tales of the Talisman; 2001; Yellow Bat Review; World Wide Fan Club.

Every attempt has been made to be comprehensive: apologies in advance to any publications inadvertently omitted.

Interior art previously appeared in Baldie and Dreamberry Wine.

"If the Doors of Perception Were Cleansed"

no queue for once so on impulse
I said let's go for it Elaine
wasn't bothered but I insisted
the time machine shuttle was
an eyeblink really we were
there like a dodgem car where
no one bumped you smooth silent
as that and Future World I was oh
I can't describe it lovely not
way out or surreal a bit like
how I'd feared somewhere you'd
make silly mistakes show yourself
up look stupid small not a bit of
it just like today only nicer and
futuristic how it ought to be the
best of home only better smoother
cosier somehow if we didn't have
to get back jobs to go to and
Elaine's mum and the kids and anyway
at future prices everything my
only complaint so dear I'd've
wanted to stay forever as it was
though Elaine was getting fed up I
knew I insisted we stay till very
last shuttle back that's how just
by accident I think I saw who runs
it now oh now all night I feel
itchy I'd wondered how whoever
made it made it so perfectly to
seem as if it was just made for
and everyone else in the street

who'd been before us says the same
we were the last to go no kids to
make us rush soon as it opened it
seems to everyone made just for
them just how they'd dreamed they'd
like tomorrow to be made to be now
all night I think awake though
I've said nothing to Elaine who
sleeps as always very well not
wanting she goes mad if I do
waking up by me how in the walls
their ancestors are taking notes
small scratchy tiny droppings
on every word and breath and
deed and thought of me Elaine and me
to know just right just how to make
up there our good clean perfect
family individualised haven heaven-ready
and promise to Elaine in sleep we will
not ever go again until I know we will

Billions to get one going there

shipbrain didn't like it tried
hard hard hard to deter but couldn't
in end override command would after
all affect only astronaut skin any objection
involving sociological aesthetic etc factors
not more than sketchily available in
programming no health risk not here sterile
environment and mediprogrammes advancedest
Sendworld's finest docskills could provide
and so and so would do did is done is on
right forearm can look at any time remind
self over and over if needed strengthen
determination on if-when return as sewn
lips though maybe not proof against scop
truth drugs whatever still would try would
try and there on arm forever now words data
bank'd found him said were oncelive poet of
once-state the THE America in Americas says
"Travellers between worlds are mute" didn't
bother to add rest where said "they cannot
tell us what they know" it was not case of
that but would not WOULD NOT they were gladly
welcome to all sensors took in all shipbrain
stored samples be content be content greeds
wannabe voyeurs with that oh be content leave
free to be own too own to share onemate Space

Or Give Suck to Whole Oceans

"songs about the shape or shapelessness of life"
(description of Kurt Weill's work by
Russell Davies. R2 July I 1999)

is dirty earthy smell of undead and how grey
bra strap but has to keep adjusting or will
interfere with how bra gets signal off Global
Positioning Satellite and you need that GPS
knowledge all every second sleep and waketime
to be safe or anything like and scratches at
again goes greyer and around stiffface other
women plan words will say to each other soon
as meeting breaks must be held to tell men is
cruel and unusual plan to nanosize intelligent
life to settle other planet just found cheap so
small to sand but what of their mothers must
exist and if ever come home what will come home
to and whisper only but when proper people go
Out There the little 'uns will get up into
all your clothes your openings and again she
pulls her bras straps shape the grey on it is
moving surely something moving now in her hair
it's smelling smiling saying nothing Mother Eden

Now it is Ours

There are no such things as 'legitimate targets' (Peace campaigner)

DEEP	truth	hurts	most
as	near	as	dammit
we	always	hunters	seek
dig	down	whorelike	pockets
we	under	go	empty
never	fills	with	lust
find	drowned	skeletal	loves
ourselves	dry	dust	hopeless
in	beings	without	rebirth
old	soldiers	meaning	corpses
alien	green	dreams	rising
cities	emptiers	of	tomorrow
here	returned	perfect	paradisal
on	monstrous	bug-bright	survivals
red-dust	rightful	revenants	returned
Mars	owners	demanding	worldwide
our	landing	squashed	forever
realler	on	us	martyred
'they'	superhuman	become	united
said	resultant	entity	reliquidises
Mother	Mars-bred	raped	GOD-BIRTHS

The Cartworth Moor Annunciation

going down some Loathsome Road
is dreaming out that natal
cleft accessible aliens come how
promised us would be here
for us not just backlit
silhouettes beamed ex altiverses all
that how ghosts playact but
close enough to touch to
really truly listen to how
we see our needs soft
claws safe indrawn pats' paws
of the gods and look
between grinning towering over foxglove
skeletons eyes soft blur where
thistledown lights sticks comes out
first from between spread traveller
legs oh and with first
what in human would be
wait for breath soundless broadcast
of light fuses fieldwalls tenmiles
to black glass proud father
or maybe is whole hive
splits sky whoopee in reply
of jog maybe too late
maybe would've preferred pray at
a distance as swallows waste
not want not into self
umbilical and mother with it
crying tail of lifegiver life
with luck it won't be
long will corrupt soon be
impure as us our air
our ruined place sent so
first message said to save

Otherland

no need for dogs to listen
or go walks have thrown sticks
here people come and go at summons

no need to pack to wait to sit
compressed between noises to get away
here door hidden by your cupboard's clothes
takes one step to anyworldwhere you wish

no need to regret
years of your face don't fit
what you want to be do who you want
here you set your age to suit your moodneed
any time any day minutes with Alicemagic pill

no need to spend day on day
season on season year on year
vain the attempt to conquer
garden train to look as wish not
outgrow revert to jungle
here just speak to plants they obey as soldiers

no need to forever discover clothes always wrong
for it weather goes by contraries rains
storms hails winds when you needdesire
to be out to walk to explore
always bright beautiful fresh warm
out when inside traps you entasked
here just set weather house figures make is so outside

no need be always the one person yourself
sumpsick of stuck as tar in memories of all wrong lost missed
heartenvy bird flies over free cat runs nightfox wisps tree
great unthought or want to ride other thoughts in other
mind have thoughtview elsewhere any but your own
here matchlight easyspeedy go be such all else come safe back

Back After Long Year's Out

bones bendy stretchy
spider plant stems
with luck will flower

eyes red spots
afterburn of too many suns
thinks those he meets

will all co-operate
to save each other's lives
how crew to meteor-impact leak

rational response
expected not found decided
weak emotions dangerous

how stowaways threaten
integrity extent result
of mission must for good

be jettisoned out airlock
glitter exploding petals in
vacuum lunge sprung out

too weak to stand pains to sit
lies in empty vacuum of home place
debriefs himself an interface

how life how art
till barbot throws him out
hostility growing how conflict

how endgame
could follow this cold forever
ice here staring down earth-trapped.

Error Error Your Work Cannot Be Marked

on screen realtime teacher
sets next test to describe
belief in Creation I key
in how two moons truth
is are breasts of goddess
gave my red home life
am marked Fail Retake is
Creation myth of Home World
have been taught should spit
baok instead spit out what
is dead gene great grand-
-parents' place to me I
do not know or care
what lies are true there
their far-off school is Past
to me is stupid how
can Earthies know anything is
use to me just because
say they know Everything
how can they know who
never came where my life
began only your swift breasts
visible but I know you
are there Mother save me
from these lies this evil
free me us from Them
we born again pure unsinning
Mother with your milk rays
blind them keep us from
their sight their sending Home

Sure As Dreamers Are

leave it alone she screamed
hitting cleanerbot frenzy
hurt her mouse-small fist
clench it's MY bed its MY
dust ball giant under it it
will WILL soon SOON turn to
like teacherbot said Earth
did first turn into planet
out of dust is promised me
wish when milkteeth went is
sure where I can go escape
no no more bossy horrid like
you machines only real like me

Seen But Not Heard

"O saisons, o châteaux,
Quelle âme est sans défauts?"
Rimbaud

immortal wind of elsewhere come
as snake oil through all space

passes girdling round this world
asking of seasons as they change,

enquiring of black or green castled hills
"are you entity I seek, the One

has escaped grinding mills of sin
or sense of same, the which is better still?"

we cry, gesture for attention, plead but
though passes over through around us

overwhelming presence everywhere has never
asked even one of us once the question

we daily nightly overhear to fever dream
and waking destroy will; must think us

too nothing to have sense soul
intelligence enough to understand to ever

be worth seeking out for answer sub-children
mindless parasites of this our planet's

greater truer beings, leaves us feeling
so utterly small we in despairing end

prepare the weaponry to somehow anyhow
destroy all the being honoured with

unanswered ultimate of questions though
to do so mean we also must destroy

along with black-white green-pink
brown-yellow red-gold seasons along with

shatter-stoned breast formed pine-spiked
castled hills look down on us and all the rest

where our feet stand and where we breathe
and where the being coils a serpent in our stars

to block our view or shadow all our lights
and burn our very air and kill ourselves

ah but as all goes to the fire surely
fan will see will know we too know

sin and how is cured will to our gestures say
"there, now; i notice you, forgive you, now go to sleep!"

We Are Also Keys to the Experiment

complaining a lifeless planet
withers our needful empathy for other life-forms
without permission the exobiogeneticist
has released onto Mars surface
snakes bred russet-red for survival camouflage
in case just in case with monster multifiltered
lungs to breathe
in hindsight the russet we suspect aesthetic
and fangs megafangs manipulated into drills
to search subsurface water out that too late we learn
in this low gravity will also grow
to immensities miles-long
their twisting piling mating bodies
churning against horizons bigger than tornadoes
red coils aping lumbering Earthside
sunsets and their clouds

how can we have sympathy for THESE
fear yes or envy
anger that they go so free where we
must creep helmeted crawl into harness hatred

that this world so loves them accepts them succors them

lustfire at their giant matings
shaking of hills to dust

our plans are made
do not tell them
soon we will seize
the scientists who made them
peg out full filled with poison

let them kill in the act of feeding

every rival god to us for Mars they made

Integrating the Stranded Alien Into Society

I have taught the being to sing
so far it sings two sharp notes repeated
the sound gave the blackhead Great Tit its name
I have taught the being to walk
So far it slithers endlessly through any
cranny it can discover as does the weasely ferret
I have taught the being to draw
so far it scratches shapes of pure pain
on every surface I value even my child-woman
I have taught the being to talk
so far it mouths forever non-stop
as TV as madman as if sound would spoil purity of act
I have taught the being to kill
so far it persists endlessly in believing
all the targets I choose are artworks to befriend
I have taught the being to love
so far it copulates as the circle
snake imperturbably within hollows of itself
I have taught the being to be human
so far it has done nothing right not once
learning too well the lesson in essence I, we,

truly not in self what should be

over its golden eye-orbs a glimmer as of halo
my eyes persist in trying to decode to read
to make spell out the words against mv teaching

“HUMAN IS AS HUMAN DOES"

Treating of the Outwearing of Welcome

Imagine a snowflake
in a polystyrene dress
bones of rich red silk

you better imagine you
won't meet them they
have made their hq

a rich walled suburb
a senior citizen's defended
solar city plan to mingle

admitted freely only with
elite leaders are here after
all traders for artifacts

what may appear as savage
makings to fashion-seekers
of oldculture empire so

often do and what could you
or you
or you offer even your
trashlitterdump only become

art when massaged breath of
dominant culture adorns with
imprimatur gains value only

when concept of megaprice
attached ah but when all goes
wrong when from sky such

thrown out when find their
money worthless their
weapons don't work here

fail fall fall
down among us ah what pleasure
melt 'em soundless screaming down.

show 'em where
real Earthlife at what
pain core of real people's art

oh wish wish in arms so sixfold
as hurled from highbalcons overlook
low worlds had pulled our rulers with

They Always Think They Know

peering in turn at
smoke-stained high-cornice ceiling
at dirt-on-dirt carpeted floor
anywhere but eyes he addresses
explains half-whisper so They won't
hear how Jupiter is hollow he heard
it on foreign late night shortwave
radio never knew which station
they never tell you and inside
contains double of each of all
other planets Twin Mercury Twin
Venus Twin Earth Twin Mars and so
and so right out to Twin Planet X
we haven't even found out visible
double of call it Planet Arthur for
example could be sleeping there on
ice and anyway at a signal some time
any could be next five seconds could
be a million years signal could be
anything maybe only dogs bats insects
maybe nothing on Earth will hear or
maybe whole air will ring we'll all
know too late to prepare will
replace all worlds with the doubles
doubles of everything on every one
will take our place and we and we all
we all life will go into that sphere
that chasm inside Redspot giant instead
and we'll never know a thing
has changed maybe he says they did
it yesterday maybe years ago maybe
all the sky the stars the sun we see
not that you see stars now so much

light we make that makes fooling us
easier he said it's all a trick They
fooled us fooled us easy as candy
from a baby he said what I'm waiting
for is when those in charge of Them
do they care what They do I don't
know anyway for a joke or is in rules
and regulations of how universe runs
which I heard this scientist explaining
on this station crackled a lot foreign
They interfere you know do the same
to Them that's what I'm watching out
for happening he said when it does I
don't know how I'll know but I know
I'll know I will I'll be the only one
- time to get away let him get on
with it with finding another listener
time to catch up on Wholedark warning band

Given Access to the DNA

long ship of bones clung under
museum ceiling now would've worn
crystal-plumed wings fireclaw tongue
will spearhead first furious vast
planned patrol over storm of Jupiter
reborn with promise for obedience
service will be let return to Earth
safe said we're sure will never
survive task of impossible we set
no more than scientists believe
rode comet down to reach us once

An Unseen Epic

his sword has happy name
now, Shoulder-Carver,
baptized in rare blood

lessers mutter it
unreal victory, slaying
Sleepers in their dream

ah but the priests say
demons in them ever wakeful
see through closed lids of ice

and did he not enter metal
cave of sky castle alone, how dare
doubters claim the fight not terrible

grim struggle of sleepwalkers
cold around him stiffly
seizing grappling

bucket helms fearsome as ail
old death combined
have we not hero now

brightness to lead us
cut necks to adorn saddlebow
sword with name that all must know

is that not joy enough
to lure ripe girls into the furrow
to set plump crops to growth?

News of the Golden Age

timetraveller is well-cultured
knows answers of best words of past
lurks shadowed at prophetess' fume-
dazed shoulder tripod-perched in
worrisomely precarious balance across
entrance to crack to dark of deep
limestone earth and when next
questioner announces self as Lyris
says the blackouts memory loss worry
her asks what she does when so so often
drunk he whispers prompting answer
as cribbed off Martial "same as sober only
better blowjobs" and cackles laughing till
hooded cone joins in and she who has had
answer not seeing funny side but feeling
in sacred place you must do as voices of
high allknowing ones do laughed wide
mouth too her bright teeth catching
some bent echo of sun outside cavemouth
far above and three were one until
his time ended snatched in spin of silver motes
straight back into nearforward of our time
lab was asked what had been learned and
choking giggling at last sobered enough
to say have found how true poem is
timeless communion of shared eternal
meaning and wrote report exact to fact except
no mention how against all rules implanted
external data and booked down next week to
go again to the same placetime enough
minutes later to meet in dark passage
backwards towards the sun Lyris after
her answer a satisfied customer on
high road to an emerging future shaped
precisely and with care how poets do

The Sanctity of His Mission

kissing her as you would a corpse
distant with loss too far
to call back even for a final
settling of overdue accounts

that is the curse of being the first
worse even than the last
the risk of contamination
the knowledge started

that will tapeworm throughout
and alter beyond resurrection
but how dare turn down the
gift made to a stranger

luckier than chance would allow
how clever-well the beings here predicted
his behavior made all due
allowances for culturefactor extrapolation

before
sending the virgin to her doom
who otherwise would have anyhow within
a cycle gone into ground

a crop-source-placator she
at least now will not have to
burrow down alone: a hybrid in
her belly, a tasty

extra bonus for the god or gods.
With luck, the slyer silver elders whisper,
the alien flesh and blood might be
even in a small bit enough to poison off

the gift-demanders: only the eldest
worship-leader of all dares wonder
what happens if it or they should get
the taste

best keep the Earthman just in case
they need to breed such spicy foreign
offering again next time
in case plain food no more enough

he's glad to be of ignorant service
hoping his child in time
will rule
this place

What You Can Do With Your Colony

missteer the ship a while
up a star, down again...
wake some colonists, thrust in,
put em to freeze again...
feud with ship computer then
find it's your only friend...
feud with your captain's
brain just because it's human...
count the years, the waste...
divide one by the other

Icarus Legion Decade One Report

"Greater than the God who creates is the God
Who knows when to pause"
Lord Jacobowitz

they I won't dignify with giving name
use seems minielectronic maybe by now nano
control weaponry we being defense of what
is best of species against onrushing of
dehumanization leave in place primitive base
brain needed to operate autonomic nervous
systems don't want to damage flight skills
too much thought but alongside as higher
decision process you might call in old
freudismus terms ego superego bred skull bit
larger to fit in and human as it were pilot
brain bit smaller but still truly one of us
oh beauty beyond compare that battle dance
as swallows hawking air currents of an edge
across such sunset sky statistics proving
just what common sense what truth of species
capability must demand edge in odds enough
worth betting on so we do we do them us and
now best of all we have true neutral eyes
to watch keep score come from who knows cares
where so long's they do not spell the fun is
surely harming no-one and soon we're promised
they'll save rehome higher human thought -
- machine of flesh when bird companion weapon
platform dies which doesn't hurt at all and
our psychologists are sure not one will die
of grief at losing first host twin lower
brain or certainly much less than proud heroes
die in combat high so high still singing flying

The Ship Commander's Subtext

take no
thought how soon who
you leave Ground-down will turn
old, dead — rejoice in freeze tanks girls
will thaw

Civilisation Counselling Service

> *"They cannot be considered human. They prey on humans. They do not prey on each other. That is the difference."*
> George Romero

    what opportunities these night-beasts waste
of flavour to never ever
    tear each other shard from giblet

    how do they know until it's tried they wouldn't
prefer each other's suffering shrieks to
    mere dull moangroans of such as us under the claw

    best of all don't they know if they took
it out on each other instead of lesser
    beings they'd feel at least

    ten feet taller in the eyes of
their mates their kids their
    otherwise-unshuttable carping mothers-in-law?

    and if none of these reasons work well
can't they waken up enough to take this one on board
    races that spare their offspring never

    grow up
Human
    at all

We Are Not Alone On Xenophon

They say you must wait in the grave
mouse-quiet Job-patient
for God to come to judge you
we have a problem here
that when Judgement cornes
it will uncover preemption
Every one we bury in this world
is up-dug wrenched to shreds
spattered like candlewax by morning

Keeping watch we hear
but we do not see
the result is always the same

We contact those who sent us
who advise searching the
UV the IF spectra
They forget we no longer know
what any of these things mean
and even if they told us

They forget in crashing we lost
all instruments save only the Contacter
safe in the Far-speaker's head

We have formed an unbreakable ring
round a grave by night
and still the result's the same

We have stood on the grave
and it has seemed the grave itself
cast us aside to erupt content

What does it search for
this unseen horror?
it does not eat, just spoils. Perhaps,

I fear but dare not say
it seeks the soul to judge.

As Foretold in the Spheres

Some fear joy simple wonder stared
up as instructed but most exalting how
fierce capering prophet portent-provider
proved his truth them blessed full-filling
Threesuns' sky on instant long long forecast

From ground too small to spot viewports in
glory-great emerald topaz garnet amethyst ruby
ships flower full holidaymaker faces gloating
tour of backwater worlds as picturesque as
promise and just right length of time to see

before to meals to gaming dance nor ever knew
they did all things just how an unwashed savage willed

Where Offering Must Precede Voyage

Half-chewed flesh remains orbit loose,
heads grin, afloat, alone, blind holes peer;
Cheshire mog, gnarled gryphon, virgin hornface,
spoiled, deadly, mutant, ape black grace
of Emptiness attendant on high shrine they tend.

Price paid, culled crew boost on wordless
as if they never had young shipmates lost
to What or Who is judge-allocatrix of voyage luck.
grim silence hiding in each head "This time
it was not me; oh Thank It offering pleased."

Returning, test is less of closeness, loyalty;
inbound such shipsters as custom now allows
pay bloodprice in fleshfall of alien prisoner -
- guests, flavoured one human-only lot picks out

Earthbound are never told of this: what business
could it be of theirs who glue themselves to
ground that must be paid to passage out to stars:
blind accidents take blame to lubbers for god-deed.

Being Asked To Explain Your Perfection - 3000 CE

Take thought to what you see
Repeats all space around what
I there is spread over as does
Light whole realms above below
Leave on for aftercome what IS
Ecstatic overload such is ALL
NOW Interfacing In to vision
I as is within vein nerve cell
Upbursts of bright within how
Make separation of bomflesh

From enhance upon enhance
Upwards from microest nano
Tribes I feelsensesee go
Under skin through artery
Rebuild me secondwise perfect
Expand all consciousness enable

Defy agegravlty wings swirl me
Round round moon-high spires give
Essence in all-vision comets
At my beckon swim-sing under
My all-system-wide what call them
Imagine tall-feet travelthrusters
Now show my net catch stars call
Grins of black hole my mirror

Let me see myself except Is
Only one flaw all such wonder
Now over lightyears all is me-shaped
Everywhere Is nowhere no Other to hate/love

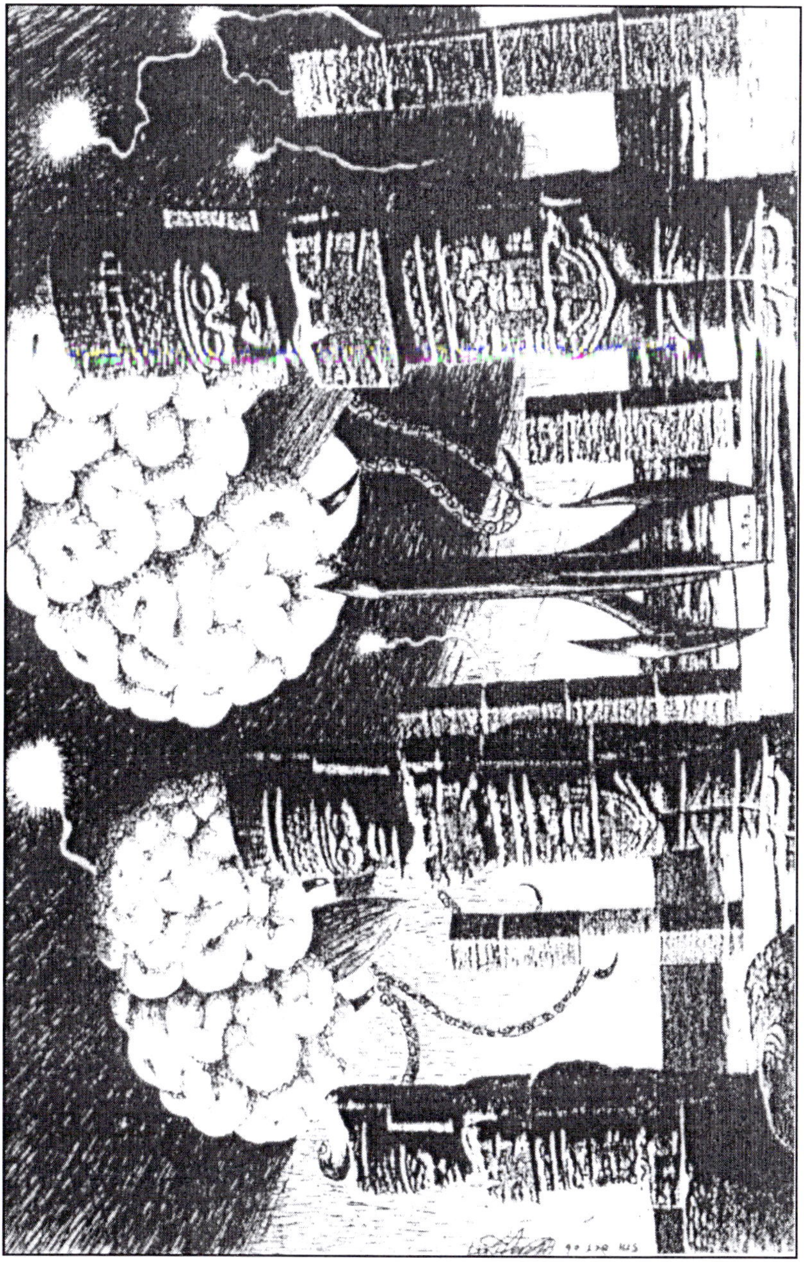

Never The Less

senders said ship's
brain young woman's killed self
not who

we named ship for
her lost grace Kosmoteira She
Who Saves

world we landed
very last has such wise one rook
mind-speaks

knows inward self
of ship guide speaks us male -
why lie?

A Balance Of Forces

I look through those eyes
scratch and fiddle at ears
don't belong to me but seem
fitting sharptip as elven
come of dark mounds of dead of
dark space where stars breed
flying barrow-tomb decide in
this day will squash emotion
fear hate rage reason will
rule will seven years as but
a day do such things as know
not will be wonders all those
heaps those hills undone of
things should do so long have

been done before will be
beamed up away complete will
set me free and then reminded
not just how thought to be
free self human as should be is
empathing with buried bit what
wants to be what it could be is
therefore sneaking in from
shadow from night-tree branchtap
of emotion is wrong therefore
this at last for once decided
to be logical getonwithit day
but also opening what comes
through door a tongue of what
pretends to be real of surface
earth not below above how even
borrowed eyes i look through
thoughts i think through ship
they ride could split world how
claphands you burst bag of crisps
still cannot switch off other
that is others screeching inside
teaspilling kicking unseen table
nearly bursts right foot to know
how boldly folk will go to get
you down and in reply words not
what you need not tractor-destructor
beam not enough to take me out
beyond their space their time to
beam past up over primitive undoing
and scratch my ears again almost
to blood and find twin peaks of
reason going going oh unutterably gone

Mars - Last Generation

fill dead moonlets
shove in everything
we ever were

attics of our race
laugh now they whiz our skies
safe place

burden has lift-off
up with drying sun
meaning unanswered

some other things
can come can solve
puzzle of us we couldn't

how we dance
now last task
shelved as if done

you after
would say
grasshoppers have best

of ants when if
no winter
ever come

we say
which sounds as well
tomorrow

without
us
comes

Last Look, Granddad's Place

pluck off floor severed toenail crescent
clung among mouseballed tracks, infrag feed, dulleye dirt —

held opalshine against grime-crack window face,
catch in smallness throughlight silver, twist as if new hurt —

wonder to see fine self reflection in such opaque-look shred; turn
round and turn from dull ray-gate to caster of shadowspurt —

seems to take silhouette I knew and place on wall between paler
where dead great and great-great holes were and

plunges place back to live-here use: as if bites hurl
man-cuticle remain back onto floorcoat feet-sticker

time to move, go — rush out, not even shutting unfitting
plasweed door and eyeholed screen still last pale ions

of insectcution power and curt as fear "Good-bye" into
black door mouth and off in hours yet to depart queue but

so much could go wrong or tumbleweed trip break leg and
make forever and eyeprickle surely in grit in breeze hotter'n

still air is never for world had childhood once and
mustn't forget cover up cover eyes head all against

dull heavy horrid near-nova sunshine girds dump
must cut all dead web strands hold to leaving Home for good.

As Is Written in the Emergency Manual

we are suffering airloss... we do not wish to believe
It is the work of uncaring universe or our own
carelessness patiently we prefer to believe our boss

Airless Extraterrestrial Enterprises tests our faith
will at very last possible instant as we hallucinate
flake into non-sentience save us reward such loyalty

with starworlds of our own goldengardened flesh-ringed
welcoming to at long last our true selves reshaping no
longer crush-deformed to small hard things facing vacweight of space

The Chosen Not Gladly

If we live past our
planet something in us still
will cry for snuffle of
waves coming for cool coo
of pigeons preening for snow-white
mountain fingernail jagging up will
take no cognisance as home
of diamond worlds of whirling
comet tails we ride of dimness
drifting dark matter our shroud

Agent Sophia

tumbleweeds Backtime: caught
on Atlantis Fence, she dons
fish-scale mask, sheds nuke

Evacuated From the Zone Two Decades On

i could pick your teeth
a train's length away
eagle on your tall
panelled courtroom wall scream to
warn too late then tear
your smug head off and apart
i could and you would
never know it's me too small
too dirty sure to
be god but why should i waste
power on old men
so many circling years gave
living on poison
ground when schoolgirls are what i
really need it for
twisting their thighs to heat a
full dark field apart

For Those We Owe Everything, Nothing Is Too Much

the time of year again is
nomansland a season we have learnt well upon

this land whose months spell out in turn
all bad emotions now is the time all chasms

open like bowels and airs turn all
from sicklysweet to acidsour just

enough to burn words away from
our songs mountains a week ago

were in nine rainbow coats of
sniffglue snow now shed to spread

curves sensuous maddeners with birth
of longing then having gotten

us off guard out of the dark falsewelcome
pores rise up pure fumes that hate us

almost as much as now ten decades
localtime trapped upon this colony

anus of the universe we hate ourselves
such mugs for coming told we were on

our way to make a brave new cycle
proper future eden for mankind

turned from idiots of the mind only into
wrecks throughout we only who survive

on all fours mostly or all threes or twos where
limbs are lost or curled back into lumps

like warts only fingernail clippings
of the great hand of the great expedition

gigantic we were and equal to our task they said
as saints and angels to conquer heaven

ah but their voices cry out still from
rare overripe organic tapes Home still

drops down on us occasionally which in this
climate change into parasites eating

ears and eyes even as we scan for content
"you did your Duty and you did

it well" only sometimes tearing ratvine
from each other it takes three to pull

clear the suckers in our weakened
end-of-line condition we wonder if in fact

our work a joke taking this place
before the aliens could like Home says yes but

perhaps really the aliens spent
a fortune mocking up this dump

to lure the best and bravest of our species
out here to sink up to the crotch the brain's

crotch even yes and doubtless
Home went along with it knowing full well what

better way to rid
the old homestead of our dangerous

glorious restlessness: for the general good
we agree of course or would if we'd been asked

A Shared Conclusion

> *"she realised because she had ESP she could never have the kind of fun ordinary girls had."*
> (cover blurb, **The Girl Who Saw Tomorrow**)

she saw him coming
deep inside his nervetrees she knew
before he ever knew
what his explosion was about to do

she knew how to deal with it telekinesis
the whitecoats had taught her when they studied her
what to call her the parameters of her talents
they had told her that was within her repertoire

showed her what something in her already knew
skill in moving over short distances elsewhere
any small object something went flick
in her as muscle tense as spit that was it

before the desperate strong as fleas
blind agile swimmers even began to enter
her warm dark private space she turned moved them
elsewhere their salmonleap he gagged

in profusion sickened disgusted horror swallowing
choking spewing hotsweet salt porridge flood
of his joy's outflow then the bright nervejumps
in his brain clogged with little whitebright

wrigglers his eyeballs filled to bursting from
within nose sinus intestine next they even
swelled as pus does the raw kibe where
chilblain ulcerated on his heel all at once he

was hive
of million of his own sperm hurled back
in on over under everywhere of him
he screamed all systems of himself

distorted to point of dying certain
total malfunction the lungs swallowed up
the brain engulfed in between
her tears she was laughing shrieking

no ordinary girl she howled
could ever've helped you really truly
love yourself to bits
too heavy the mess to teleport away

beyond her weight/power ratio had to
roll out slimed herself from
bursting from under but at least
need not travel to the shower

bringing to herself
fine spray from rain
outside to wash off all
the fun she hadn't had

At Last the Übermensch Has Come Out Into the Open

pulling his brain from
inside from tower overlooking trying
hard to think for him but only
dragging memories round and round as
old horse machining grain and slowly slowly
how does it happen being sucked in being
turned round looking up up from the plaza
to one standing on highest parapet a spot
take to his mind the truth the high place
is not gateway to the kingdoms he has not
power enough to change any of us from inside
only enough to wake us to what we've got
isn't it time he accepted defeat isn't
it time oh god stepping into air
trying to fly falling trying all the long
way down to splat to put inside one any
mind of the watching crowd enough
of self to go on living
on is taffy-pulled his brain now on
the pavement tendrils out in all
directions each running almost
nearly reaching to touch
each still shining watching unmoving
crowd-member's pair of feet
who each delicately step back
just enough to avoid contamination
of the ooze of brain and only
halfway down the monster edifice
one single dirty scabby
city pigeon eyes a little red begins
counting the crowd one by one marking
each face for later one by one

Grinding Through the Routine Like a Mountain Pass

it was not well timed
the coming into lifeform of the alien being
arrived sweet as honey into brain of similarly
woolly fourleg stood up Huck Land chewing over
old A62 a silver snake far below under Pule Hill
and goddamnit at once knew too late fixed in
situ to move to another host in the slat-sider
truck that moves there so small so distant
comes to collect it - us - to go to
slaughter and well after all to hell
came here only to tell the bastards
run this planet we are onto them
and as if it matters deliver final warning
before out of the god-shape clouds
we swoop and finish them goddamn
wish i could in time convert this
sheep i think the masters here call it
to transmit distress signal to godeffit
bail me out in time
still in the meantime my last time
beautiful to look down on
as if from our rockets' gunports
on the bare shedskin land
almost like looking in on down on
cleverer father dying

Translation Station

our holoprojections mine the alien's
meet in neutral space vacuum doesn't harm
holoprojections let alone equally neutral
transparent though sparkly sprightly shape
envelope swirls about at edge of vision
translation machine Old Ones sent to make
sense of this meeting:preprogrammed talk
began, "I" said pleased to meet him her it
they the 3 heads of being each acknowledged
politely tones ranging scratched chalkboard
fingernails to honey falling into toffee
translation machine gave each different
homey accent Tyke Noo Yaawk Strine consensus
statement how brave "I" was to show self in
public without prosthetic replacements for
2 heads sadly lost in whatever terrible
accident full sympathy did hope no such
loss universal in "my" species or worse still
plague effect radiation punishment would make
"it" weep enough to drown. At this point
silence fell prepared line on each side
exhausted and signal transmission delay
for instructions from higher up kicked
in but no prob none thanks to translation
machine prevented embarassment of angels
passing talk-gap busked it telling simul
in languages of both sides how wonderful
the making of machine itself the wonders
greater still of who made it and how with
complete specifications met and as still
some hitch delaying further things to say
passed as ok by backHome committees on both
sides machine then sang improving song of
hopes of universal understanding in all
innumerable tongues it knew at once a feat
so painful deafening mindbattering both
at once holos imploded that was the end
of that however looking on the bright
side agreement is made a constructive start

Adaptation Feedback Blues

under artificial skies
dark roof of his mind
about as likely I'll reply
as Moon is since we left
webglitter rain does its
downwindow racetrack tricks
just how you'd think real
thing would do or did back
when whenever it was it
did wherever that was this
world in prethis form or
some other we pretend we
remember remembering and
whatthehell great thing
is he thought he thought
we're extremophiles life
like us survives extreme
environments fake as year
effing dot or since anyhow
and nothing answered back

"Intellect Without Opposition Stagnates"

weary of worlds are global cities
too many this trip but this system
at least from distance something

extra to see faceted beam back
reflect light different colour
binary suns computer provides

metaphor always answer when
can't think how to describe to self
what see fix in memory sweet she

voice they gave it says anciently
what were called Mecca dance halls
had revolving globes cast just such

effects on couples moved to music
below i was happy then i know what
to think even if unlikely chose

to add description of effect to
report would transmit irrelevant
of course look of places only use

might have for trade balance of
power species strong enough a
potential threat all that what was

supposed to put in let her i call
it her word all that but if against
odds i wanted input this sight knew

now what to say decided next space
port one of these even perhaps if
had facilities would decorate ship

front effect of lipsticked mouth
would face for her to match
her voice my partner now in dance.

Just Like My Nan Said

hedgehogs in my childhood could
easy under the silver spilt of moon
lift rotten apples hugely on their spines
i never saw it but i know

has to be so and so i know
this spaceship i drive now
can on its turrets trap
asteroids all round our flying town

it has to be and if it isn't
so, so what, I'll never know and they
who sent me out to do the impossible
can pick me sometime squashed out of their way

just as the last back Home
in the last roadrace round
the last unshattered highways did
the last hedgehogs around

the very last of tidying up
they did before the ships
opened their bays and all but gently
swallowed survivors

Is Sure Proclaimed a Public Holiday

chasing bus is carrying him away

under sky white metal plate
thought twinned one some secret
war'd put in his head has to be
all round silence cuts off
world as if in Taliban Central
silence heads turned away wd
be ideal if had chosen but not
imposed as this this is No-Win
City was sure full of weightfulness
fell all on him all rest floated
away as hot air balloons grace into
escape only on him weight as Pink
Panther cloud rain only down for
him sees woman smiles she shows
one swift swing of split-tight
skirt is glitters in intensity of
light serpent down from waist sure
not seeing things next street is
red crag farmer faces squashing
between hands feet to death thin
white suits of plains would agree
should be done but frightens to
see all the same must plead for
safe asylum this hospital here is
likely if anywhere though expects
will turn away feels nuisance to
be inferior hypochondriac and in
any case this silence will not
here anywhere hear him is cool
Reception although knows beds wards

will from past remain Unearth warm
is amazed is not kept waiting is
greeted with awe "You are the guy
contacts the Beepee elementals, that
crystal of the sea crushing through
the brain is pain you bear for all
to save us all, oh come in, welcome"

that is when he really runs like hell

The Alien Uses the Earth As a Corpse Dump

your mountains hide me in their rain,
only the crazy saw my ship come down:
you are so violent, bandit-tribal, blame
will go to you when she is found I
tricked before the act to give herself
look just like one of you saying our
mating journey here should be as little
obtrusive as our three moons into song -
she did not even sense intention when
I sang the old favourite one laments
how stranger's fate is to die far from
home... I leave small tokens of her life,
such personal treasures as some jackdaw
of you will steal, be found with, prove
motive you will assign to this will fit -
for my true reason, in a thousand years
if you should meet us I'll have left
what fully will confess which by then
you might know enough to sense its sense -
till then, the one who suffers for me has
for consolation that as far as I have
faith I will believe he is divine in

The Sins of the Children

taste of metal
pain aoross chest
limbs pinneedled
as sex too long
as heart attack
as panic attack
is no cause only
other of future
post-human comes
inside you short
visit to know
what has outgrown
nostalgie de la boue
will leave you will
leave what was as
was unchanged only
forever after you
will have no
content only blind
of alcohol between
sense and thought
or sex or noise or
screens of images
or endless thud
of beat or speed
beyond all safety
or machines you
play play you or

any every thing
can blot an instant
out this spider
metal cities star
to star strung out
are birthright of
your far get's get
and how bar with
come armageddon far
beyond your power as
mere dull being in
ditchwater street
to wipe all descent
out can they be
stopped from getting
being becoming oh
what glory as of
dream of god you're
never to be nothing
not even yourself
again and far beyond
such time suoh space
such creatures blot
oh in such agony as
crucified across
year after year of
galacticleapfrog
light selves from selves
torn with remembering
what no longer being
you they've wholly lost

Included Out

he sends me where he does not want to go
social events parties family things
gettogethers of old schoolmates funerals
he programs me beforehand to be polite
sociable wear the right expressions
make smalltalk all those human things
he says he cannot make himself do
not successfully he also primes me never
to reveal i am not him i am his android
double i do it all well am popular get
invited back afterwards he downloads my

performance my experience experiences it
himself sometimes he is it seems jealous
of my easy access to what it is to be a
social success punishes me with electric
jolts small whips pokes slaps wristburns
such like but never enough to hurt for
long to damage enough to leave a mark and
then he cries says is sorry how grateful
he is really he i who am not human spare
him agony of revealing he who is human is
so bad at doing what humans do i never

ever tell him it is not my place how it
is tiny signs the tiniest i detect i am
sure beyond doubt more than half at least
the others at these dos are same as me are
not the humans they appear to be at all and
all the towers of the world i am so sure
full night on night of humans hiding from
each other and the nightlife gatherings the
joyful babble backslap joking people get -
- togethering even the solemn tears release
of layings down to earth to burn is really us

but then perhaps if so obvious they all
the human ones like him already know this is
conspiracy unspoken who would break such spell
what unwise word desirable to spoil answer
is perfect to such needs of all and then i
wonder briefly who or what is fooling who & then
i wish real anger were softwared into me that i
could feel as is deserved for such fool being
made completely out of me instead smile sets
in place required of course to make sure never
ever will he know i know & go ash-weary to the ball

In Reply To Your Lack of Faith

are we not still human
still say Earth Home in
same breath hold Christmas in
both hearts flesh and adapt
even would love President Who
if you ever remembered told
us name in time still
ruling there see here's proof
under these seven russet shiners
look here's shrine bright new
all round faithful-full pray
nonstop as rockets same green
godchild as you who rose
again reborn your metal Moon

.

It Depends If You Believe the Witness

Edge

on day once out of direct sun

steep old leaves slippy underfoot
maybe a late frost touch earlier
lingered shadow of this hanging

wood made them little toboggans
here and there already white
fat candies wild cheery blossom

caught head throwing up Housman
line about fifty springs too
little room to see that sight

so many grooves old trains ran
on round brain how switch points
or wasn't it time slipped and

caught against trunk ok breath back
careful steady not much further
down now to level track round

water dam held back time whatever
alien wonder came said come to
set you free you don't belong

here stranded too long almost
except deepest mind level forgot
what you really are ship waits

hidden under there where windripples
change their pattern oddly a sort
of oval interruption see between

those two trunks straight down
there the darker water is and
illusion delusion gone and worse

still had that one too often fee
before and to see an escape route
open and then shut before you

can take it fifty springs is
too much room shit on it slipped
again hummer that's bluebell's

early near full open another
sign of global warming another
well-worn groove around around

again and on the ship the alien
noting in its log in its twitter-
tongue another one too far gone

too late to retrain to be worth

Saving

The Time-Lag Grown With Distance

half-peeled browning
apple toothmarked by clumsy mouth
too impatient to scare doctor off

pictures they send us
how our world is now
true or lie means don't want us back.

Is Still Perhaps the Prelude

in ruins all alone all others
back on ship to first-sort finds
drink celebrate couple now
tomorrow we go Home

a last time idly i reconjure
holoselves who built it left
same faces same ones separate
show first then entwine two

a gloat of ghosts first smile
sweet benevolent wise recite
as music as prayer as chant
story of universe from birth

to culmination in this starfine
Allcreation World then in twin
scene must've been as proud as
sure image they sought to also

leave for any here come to find
faces feral slaver snarl tear of
helpless children of their race
heart brain twin and shape genitals

all till all gone the end THE END
a flashback Wordsworth to Stonehenge
saw same splitbrain in ghost Druids
flowertongue bards sicklehand killers

ah but where where the girl back
beggarpoor her soldierman dead fellow
wanderer of emptiness out of war in
Amerikay came to distract doomdoubt

show him we do we can we must go on
whatever happen or how bloodamp
all worlds we find and switched those
holos off and went to see if any

thighs on ship still left
not yet completely occupied and thought
the ruins falling monoliths behind
horizon as my jetbackpack leapt me on

is not our problem we only
explorer experts sent to put a set
of facts into the pool of such Home
let OUR wisemen sort for meaning

just do not in the finish turn
around and tell us what the kind
of End you have in mind for us
recarolling again Goodbyetown's

two-head's killcure Art call it song

Say When

planetborn this lot
come night after night
come slumming in our bar
come buying lots of drinks
come pretending to talk spacetalk
talk it like baby talk
see in their nostrils their Adam's
apples gills eyes you see it
movement says
we hope you'll hurt us says
we fear you won't
know when to stop

Almost An Anniversary Ritual

arguing computer HAL's
motivation fatal love vampirism
jealousy of fleshblood poet's
instinct to spanner works and
on and on you'd think real
friend hero relative lost love
argued about anything better tho
than sit before each watching door
for anyone who anyone might make a change
wondering be glad or not when
barman cuts off life support time
to get off out alone together in
eternal night all that tired and
empty emotional stuff Artificial
Poets these days do so much
better than us suffering overload
take guilt all on themselves
next will be said is was
HAL first Second Coming

A Purposing Of Loss

metal burst
from dull sky dived ground
pierced stands half-on half-in Hog
Hill priest tells

all starting
now with this one child
must put dead in close touching
hand on hold

soon enough
grip round a ring
stop from going back again
without us

Perils of the Return

be exact she
thought into me not vague
guilt show

me I must SEE
as there what you your star-beast DID
up there

put me to BEE
in there with you then she thought at -
through me

make me KNOW what
my strange sister gave gives
I WANT

The Pass Of Glory

From high mesa plumed painted horsemen stares down
into steep snow-filled pass where small fat man
one arm under cloak inside frogged uniform coat
with other arm lashes with dulled boots spurs
gaunt stumbling neckdown near collapsing
pony on through armpit-deep drills
so slowly less than walking pace on
away uphill from where
abandoned gaggle of footsoldiers huddle round near-dead
fire. Chief signals, and warriors divide, the most
going from right to end misery of tornclothedtroopers
exhausted far past self-defence: he and two others,
enough and more, turn to continue parallel on canyon
rim above little leader, curious more to see
how far he gets and will he reach summit before
they choose to swoop down to take his life or
just enslave for pain-affliction, that decision
left for now to signal, eagle or fox or condor
as maybe, from Great Spirit guide
on how best to deal with whiteskin strangers
who have air of also possessing
instruction guidance sacred from the sky.

Mechanically the exposed arm continues laying on
whiplashes to keep torn beast moving.
Equally without thought the other arm's hand
goes on rubbing at pain inside so usefully
distracts from ache of hunger.

Inside the head the brain
once reshaped Europe led again out of
captivity to so nearly conquer all again
so cunningly, defeated, slipped away,
so cunningly disguised as serving maid so
ugly chose to hide her boil-marked face,
over damp fields inside junk-loaded warrefugees'
cart to port to bribe with gold sewn into
undergarment lining to get sail set and safe
past all Perfide Albion's seapatrols
to New Orleans be himself had sold to
Yankee pedlars but enough loyal French there
still to start new army, make new Empire of
Wild West, set aside as if shrug all that,
forgot as if never existed yet another
band of men had followed yet another
of his dreams to doom; his new plan
clear as crystal of icicles on rocks above
him manlong now, a few days more and would
be at the coast and time to sail again,
to make new realm across ocean yet -
and felt already silk around his flesh
the robes of Cathay's Emperor-to-be.

Every Generation Doesn't Know It's Born

My son, why do you always complain
will you never understand
how lucky we are to live in this world
as it is when so easily
all could have been so
terribly different
you must show respect
for those who made us what we are
inhabitants of happy peaceful
times golden times
of salvation free of hardship

look you are failing in
History how badly I cannot
believe it at the parents' night
I was so ashamed when your teacher
"more in sorrow than anger" she put it
had to tell me you did not even get right
in your term exam the name or our greatest
hero of all she who saved us our people
from being wiped out made slaves
just like so many others

here put this poster on your wall
you must take down one of those
foolish singers you waste your
time your money on listening to
put it up above your bed
a permanent reminder look her
name is there in big letters
tells you how to spell it get it
right kept us free with

n

how her great victory stopped
the biggest empire Earth
ever saw in its tracks sent
them home with tails between
legs not only they never
tried again she inspired
our brothers over the seas
already defeated to
break free rise again

2000 years now
all owed to her come on
stop sulking looking
out the window listen properly
to me listen repeat her
beautiful name after me
spell it out letter
by letter
BOUDICCA

The Last Are Not The Least

Foully our fierce
lees rotate; spun
escapespeedwise, go
exward, X-ward, is out -
travel of seedsparks
spreads our demise -
- disease to ALL is
defiant or caring you
universal decide last
choice you have to make

Wise That Needs No Tent

stage act thoughtcaster
pulls you volunteer steps you
to world beyond is
where Pharaohs beyond steam-drive
temple doors into steam trains
haul pyramid blocks
leave peasants idle dry months
riots so need more
wars instead ruled world still do
is nightmare ibis-head has
you to question must
be demon spawn pain sends on
beyond to world hollow core
creatures rule pull you
into Pole to tear mind loose
shred to sparks message
out to kinthings in other
hotiron empty centre
planets your agony spreads
universe size spills
line to line back into hall
thoughtcaster rules you beg help
he laughs laughs at not
with you audience join in
swallows last neurone
flare says to crowd My fee is
safe now boots brainless you-lump
down into crowd to
tear to squash to pull apart
best night ever had

In Absence of an Acceptable Referent

These who drown in Kitezh town
sleep on in the dark under sorrow's eyelids
Velimir Khlebnikov, *Zangezi*

they go to such length to miscomprehend rip off
inner city culture fine but don't won't let thru
door as come with it huge gleamcoils serpent born
of menstrual blood such other inhabitants of Halloween
tattoo across her stubble skull the dark skull says
Fuck You in speech balloon over wingsndagger dog called
Nuke licks any balls its own others or will eat given
least chance a permanent prey drive kid ignored licks
space to see through off smeared bus windows kicks dummy
around floor to flavour to taste is hard to count how many
are of these a decade of foreboding recycled as to what
hangs nailed to door keeps out such where CCTV begins is
naive to assume heritage industry bears feet hide or
plastic mockup of what bits of Vikings flayed church
door had once could as well be pickled shark artist new
got better richer gig is mark forbidden shopping xanadu
entry with what might even recognise bits of selves will
not pass bouncer test poachers-turned-gamekeepers those
recruited off them to deter them she pass turnoff bits
of selves uncomprehending till some night called back
rejoin become all whole again some night computer clocks
all stop some night skies raining fire of serpent flight

Encountering The Future Today, Crimsworth Dean

Saltersgate ski-slope steep down
between high stone walls -
slip-stumbling down wondering how
the hell laden packponies burdened
under Cheshire salt panniers ever
made it up halted an instance weighing
up how to get over miniAlp of fallen
inward wall-stretch sensed something
approaching my back fast probably some
idiot scramble-biker jumped aside let
him break his own neck not mine and was
past hurtling on down narrow path throat
but must be seeing things not bile a
glimpse then gone sharp right from
view at bottom a sort of imagine ma-
length silver bullet and convinced an
illusion hallucination and at last at
bottom out suddenly above Lumb Falls
more impressive than expected roar and
two parts veil from below feet of side-
-stream off this slope down past larch
gold into side of pool main wider fall
poured into below rock ledges blackholed
as cave eyes and ludicrous in the pool below
twirled silver man-length a little more
maybe round and round marks on exterior
small portholes joins inserts the like
crude similarity to human floating on
back and spun and spun in near-still

waterstretch between fall and next small
rapid and thought best not stare doubtless
after microlites all these other new-
ways of getting about some new leisure
device come in or maybe some government
surveillance craft on test best pretend
to ignore and crossed bridge and started
slant up next slope unable to resist glance
or two back at what still turned round and
round and on along valley side brown
bracken to knees and on into Nat Trust
woods wondered should I ask someone report
what seen and though best not a dozen
reasons and looking across valley where two
huge glacial erratics hung on field tongue
down into metal-colour autumn goldcopper
beechwood though half-saw sliver flash go by-
whoosh on and up over Pecket Well black
hillend obelisk : ah well, doubtless it It
mattered someone else would deal with it. And
back past Midgehole lighting up time and into
small Albert towncentre pub till train time
to find among those turned an instant to stare
at outsider before back to their own local
doings stood at bar as regular as regular
stood upright now telling rest what horse
to bet each race next day looking dim bar
light almost nearly manlike this silver thing
a gain and still minding own business decided
day proved at least one thing what we need
most machines to tell us what to do take
all those decisions never stop needing taking.

The Parts To Make The Whole

Had been planet peopled, full—
as nova swelled, engulfed it,
lit it to ministar, spat it out
to travel endless to our sky,
disrupt its law with small sun night—
what remnant life firespiritwise
clings onto it comes down to visit,
rides behind dog eyes and guides
through doors and windows, entered
to observe, then act as outworld's
heat entity decides: furtive in high
iecture theater art of official hours
professor directs dissection, bizarre
reinsertion in unusual sites of limbs
and organs as chosen: few of students,
eager acolytes, worshipfully obey:
behind him on high lectern vast dark
shape rises, wavers, waits its moment
to infuse self into corpse. The dog
leaps in and up and bites—black entity
wavers, dissolves, is gone—in seconds,
before anyone can interfere, dog, vaster now,
storm-size, leaps down and takes into its
jaws corpse covered as with grain-sprouts
from Osiris with all added extra flesh
extrusions, bounds out unstoppable.Outside
it races, down through endless boulevards
as lit now, translucently, as manga witches'
skins would be, eyes saucer moons
of childhoods grown deranged. At last
it halts where as at Spider Center all
great ways converge, plaza as huge & empty
as god's tomb. Wait's no longer than three
heartbeats' thud.and swiftly as antimeteor
beast & corpse rise up as if gravity's
throat were cut, unwitnessed miracle.

Outriders Of Outward Settlement

say we emptied a jeweller's pocket
thousand stars a minute passed

my wrist-brain counts for me
no voices off any calling "welcome"

so we could blow them away
would prove what

only we have technology
could make light darkness

i say to myself they ignore
us ok ignore them turn

away from portal resume
stealthy way to sleep bays

a blind eye turned if don't make
issue officers know crackdown could mean

mutiny what does it matter
in such long-run those

sometime-to-be-colonist
women when we find a world for them

that turn and again we crew we
going to no new home

slow or swift sober or drunk
we take them memories of Home

how they shine in their sleep-time
nova on nova burning

some year on new eden sometimes maybe
will look up where we long since went

faint puzzle frown on resumed aging
lining foreheading wondering

till child husband pioneering
calls them back to real-time real

There Must Be Some Moral In It

on this cryochamber wavehand
in front of sensor up comes
message explains whwhy in
here is poet found guilty did
not write 9/11 poem sentenced
to deepfreeze unconsciousness
term till end of War on Terror
date is a K years ago no hint
in any shadow of devultured sky
of when this one's term'll end
as we leave relieved unsmiling
autoguards repeat security check

At the Heart of Nothing Business Plans

dreaming joy power to annoy
safely at some genteel-gentle
lit-type do claiming proof to
hand will soon reveal of just
you wait interBronte incest in
as many possible combinations
as moor-edge hidden pathways
woke to thuds bangs to windows
whathehell next door's garden
gone to Pennine abandoned all
heather-grown humps full bloom
now though not bright under
grey sky quarry and rust-piled it
bristled as hedgehog back with in
sort of wedged crown dead rocket
ships end of space age or USSR
stuff and how the hell got there
and to hell would worry when time
to get up too early yet to think
and thought'd teach him mock in
dream even Brontes sure after all
a coven and what powers there to
change world even dead could
even out of all stars bring all
spacemen back to visit crash
their ships in tribute to them
there and anyway good this no
longer feel obliged to go each
year see heather out in colour
here come to him his doorstep and
with that huge mess there who cd

ever even notice how his own plot
just mess setaside carbon sink he
preferred name for jungle and next
time spoke to that gathering he
thought will prove how Branwell's
biggest failure unsuccess as Fenian
spy bomber railway saboteur in
next dream side by side all battled
dinosaurs before the Flood no crazier
than blackbird gobbles hung as tight-
-rope artist till near fails off with
fatness rowan berries soon's red
ripe will curse all winter none are
left to tasty up ice times and through
such sleep reluctant to get up restart
day's do is sure hears in new quarry
new there so old abandoned in its
look hammer and chisel sounds of who
inscribing on those fallen dreamers'
ships messages just right to keep them
returned rightly down to earth old
Tyke way of cutting what sticks up
above parapet down to size Town
Rules etc or more likely just like
Haworth now guidance information done
in Japanese soon as Berlin Wall in
bits most even genuine as Bronte bobbin
off dead mills be time to turn starfaring
remnant into souvenirs wonder what
percent his neighbour'd share could
market slogan how really truly all
those loving Brontes found alive Out There

Beginning the Gift With the Word

altho such shortlives
eyeblinks against us
evidence is they nonforget
down hundreds generations

precise instance this one
holy book content precis
beamed now into wholemind
home and all colonies

clear see demands gloats
when occurs fall of
Babylon great city wicked
not pure as earthscratcher

tribe of desert edge observe
now analysed timeline is in
their planetspin calendar
well plus 2000 orbits

hear we have beetle-armoured
tribe claims mind-faithful
to words of bookwriter tribe
from over far seas

is camped on ruin of was
this same Babylon is grinding
under machine treads even
least remnant brick of

is concrete over is to do
to uttermost what book said
is recommendation destroy
such pitiless destroyers now

quick before get off planet
come our way find we build
gardens floating in sky
towers to each moon blind

tribe memory mistake our world
city BBLN born again named
target here now beam evidence
such can't defuse harmlessise

demand take out take down
threat without end seal
under tombshell all one desert
pure dead as book's purest wish

As Chosen For the Summons

told they come out from
endless sky above to set
us free as we go to
high place we are told crown of
three valleys deep as night we
wait and wait and wait
some like me wait badly itch
no inner resources
some buddha-calm squat as if
float on peat-coat fly on grass
wind waves some buy from
stalls soon spring up hauled up tracks
rivals from each of three ways
united though in foresight of food drink needs for
mementos were here
for this great day ways to spend
money time just at cusp when
even these failed when
riot disorder breakdown
of fellow feeling
shivered in air round crowd
they stepped from it there among
us all along began
to glow to sing such wondrous
things to rule the world
another time if ever
were another which I doubt
now they have us caught
forever in their spell what
need of a repeat
I would not go alone not
ever take their choice of mate

At Lunaburg As A Neutral Venue

some things in culture
genes Merchant of Venice wants
security against loan
what can't transplant brain
tries enforce courtwise though will
mean irreversible death
justice owed even
such one as too many fox
pig rat splice to be Human
laughter in court Judge
refuses hologram first
Author Shakespeare chance to speak
Merchant Mischwesen
stops jokes in tracks Megnet proof
all there all everywhere
non-Human genes in
either race did self or gift
of aliens or both is
none can give mercy

A Purpose Come to Being

I go first
for tests of stability
of humanity battery
of inkblot images
multichoices
reactions under truth drugs
so many more I can't remember
am told at last have
achieved sufficient
passmark leveis in
all categories
will be safe for me to change
will not make me
un in antihuman
whatever I become
now I can look at all
the possibilities offered
computerwise 3D alterimages
appear before me
what I could be become
would be criminal
offense worse than any alien
pornwatch even to see these
without sufficient stability
rating
horrible the indecision
even limiting my looking
to choices within my budget
precious savings of so many

drudge decades
still so many to see
take on elements of me
me of them before my eyes as
craziest funfair mirrors ah
but all so beautiful although
of course as I agreed in test
human is best still
how glorious to have
falcon wings narwhal horn
coil on coil of cobra
peacock tail catbody
porcupine panoply of
spikes mega elephant
tusks doesn't even have
to be life still exists could
be extinct stegosaur armour
terrible tyrannosaur body
I am dizzy now with
choice voices over
speakers demand decision
at last my selection
almost random did it
forget to say can also be
imagined creature is just
only just affordable very small
version of unicorn I am so
wonderful seeing myself at last
really so not simulation
let out into grassland
to find pool and maiden
will take my head into her

lap unafraid of sharp spike
before those hounds are loosed
halloo hallay to hunt me down
that end the other factor
kept the transformation price
inside my poor small range
ah worth the wonder though
of this small flower-swarded
time her soft her violet
breath her long hair
round me my eyes sweet
bed-warm her kind tears
gentlest rain I scarcely even
hear the faint far barks begin

Sticks & Stones

stripped of clothes how world
of green skin scars shiver in
meteor rain

Still More Sensitive Than a Multisensory Machine

all six senses sensored
to max datatrans back on
alien aspect trouble is
feed bypasses own brain
means self here knows no
more of Other than deaf
biind unnosed untongued
unhanded mindsoulless is
so sad greatest instant
all history was told and
all knows is own ego cut
off input world foetus
unborn old kidult angst
again even self-mirror
poet still someday back
to Base if security will
permit will let will know
through to every sense's core
if only secondhand second time
know what could have even given
different circumstance have
known loved even worshipped
then as if'd been really
there as in THERE can
plagiarise self record
event is perfect poem not
that by then old news and
all changed utterly there'll
be anyone human still caring

Inadmissible Evidence

stretched far beyond design limits
android in interrogation machine
remains silent though inside
inbuilt systems approach
overload of ecstasy
to prolong sensation however
is not sole reason machine-being
will not speak give interrogators
anything they fail to realise
fleshbrains being other side
of such comprehension gulf
no conspirator has told it anything
it knows nothing save only
secret of universe
no human wants to know

Must Ensure No Media Get This

such a typical civvy target
marketplace crowd sunsetting
out of buying into eye other
sex promenade didn't grasp
till hit didn't just fall fell
apart blew away In bits arms
legs heads hair eyes etcetera
as leaves off in all directions
were aliens fakes not human not
worth wiping at all what possible
effect disintegrating load of
third parties likely to have on
enemy morale reforming now on
far horizons go on watching us
what we do with a neverending smile

All For a Silly Game of Football

In this parallel universe
Christmas truce held and
when generals both sides
ordered own front lines
shelled to deal with such
treason clear way for fresh
troops to make fresh attack
both sides turned backs on
each other marched away from
each other went and took
the HQs and shot the generals
in lumps as you would do would
you not given the facts of it
fed faces poppy red to dogs to
cats but then this parallel
now long years after is so
cold so empty place such lack
of god of patriots of wild
girls wearing black jazzed
to forget & oh so many sadly
memorial makers broken bankrupt

Route 66 Exchange

after alien probe
she had snakes in her breath : they'd
her dreams good as tears

Trained to the Peak of Performance

"listen there's a hell of a / good universe next door, let's / go"
(e e cummings)

this was wild as a world on a windy night
girls with hissing eyes

didn't think'd appreciate even plenty his
supply ol rhubarb and custard flavor
condoms didn't look like missed
childhood these
across emptiness mid-nonair stone well
hung stretched forever had Great Wall
uprooted escaped gone walkabout orbital
Medusa got first these girls her
parthenogenetic daughters her gift to
heaven the towers were they demons angels had
had her eye on first thing made
room for herself got rid of too many
previous salvations now the wall

nearer nearer gates open show teeth tongues
stick out will land his just like cornflake
box craft on one into warm inside into
new home all round in cockpit now
girls fought tangle as snakes as toads ignore
ignore prepare welcome speech sent by Wholeearth
bring greetings brethren of another star whatever
you it they are etcetera must be his duty whatever
this was all about portholes full now of red rough
licked up spun head over tip now off into whatever
dark tunnel sensors said eyes said girls now whatever
had been eyes before hissing now sprang flowers forth
beautiful oh beautiful no earthflowers such these
whitemoons scent of blackcurrant a million times whatever
honeyheather all barriers gone now knows one with whatever

is everything is Everything if still separate enough have
eyes of own would look past flowers scents fleshwings would
see behind behindside of wall hangs over edge of Emptiness is
Whatever you ever wished whatever wanted back most of everything
is all you ever didn't get or got and lost is whatever is Most
is whatever is essence of rhubarb and custard girls is too late

Whatever everything is all about is you know you know
your know is bound to be your fault you failed to make
your speech you know who sent you did not sacrifice for this
all Earth had left of anyeverything to lift ship sent help-search
for you to be the heat ot things one with the One whatever
and still there is no help still Allyou hissings all high delight

Truce Negotiations with the Timesters

blank white eyes like portrait
busts watch you in through Town
Hall foyer try to tell yourself
vestigial organs no longer meant
to see a thing these creatures
whatever visual equivalent of
telepath term is take in whole
world around direct to synapse
still some reptile layer of own
head fight/flight reaction kicks
in & mouths look sewn up ok get
nourishment direct from atmosphere
now through skinpores we know all
this I know all this from full
briefing only dammit why you
things you THINGS you're so far
ahead of us so clever why keep
on yr outer casings souvenirs scars
horrid traces of what you were of
ogod that's worst of when you were us

Always Begin with an Exit Strategy

shave aftershave image indecision then
put on favourite t-shirt one said
"Porno is folktime's

Continuous Past gone posh" 'd be
wasted on sort of cactus-tipped

pyramid thing 'd won live contest
to be first human to meet & greet

but maybe on global linkup billions
watching some ex-litcrit colleagues'd

see with luck anyhow anyoldhow annoy
botox-stiff crap out of em bastards

and knew shd be thinking feeling some
any more significant thought emotion

greatest moment just so in human
history but of course anyone any

sense knew all a fake not perhaps
alien could really be genuine space

ship moored to ISS surely genuine so
crazy looking imagine geode crossed

with pointy hat frilly sleeve clown
outfit couldn't be human pretence

we'd've made look series deadly
serious impressive and if so alien

could be real real as this stretch
limo smoked windows all that minders

at least this part being done right
city limits receding into isolated

brownfields off towards where pro
tem interim podium arena for

encounter was more like it but sure
as dammit if real alien it wasn't

couldn't be first real FIRST meet
governments spooks'd've been all

over it like what yanks say mouthed
phrase with pride white on rice got

all secrets for sure and suddenly
moment here and oh god had forgotten

script no here it was coming up on
picture screen surgeried into left palm

and keep voice calm steady slow sound
profound sincere like rehearsal video

and half into first sentence out of
swollen green cactus bit up out of

bit of pyramid where eye'd be if was
occult symbol if was dollar bill came

couldn't tell what lightning of colours
end of worldish only much smaller ate

t-shirt and then whoosh whizzbang
pyramid flew away gone no instruments

detected and of course got all blame

As If Cities Had Time To Listen

kill all spacemen they're
diseased they must be having
gone up there where all
germs fall come from off dirty
filthy comets cries Earth Pure

Not Too Proud To Learn

maggots into wounds
eat infection leave healthy
flesh to heal unscarred
aliens learn fast eat thoughts
of humans leave perfect gods

Having Inherited Great Uncle's Time Machine

"Best before End" neat
copperplate warning control
scale bore but after
all didn't say you couldn't
go beyond all things
see what wasn't there wotthe
hell one drink and go

New Heorot Honours Its Unexpected Guest

gene-modded to eat light
brings to head of feast-board
presence of absence to our sight:
dark as the darks of darkness
silence roared how futures do

Ozymandias of Mars

Jack's giant fell up
not down off two-worlds-linking
tree slowdying still,
lasted long enough to breathe last
air, drink last water, kill world.

Cultural Interface

blue men so supple
seem boneless twist
wriggle dance around
our first settlement,
neither welcome nor
unwelcome their visits
not interfering not
entertaining no help
no hindrance not
even really here we
guess if don't believe
in them they won't
                    in us.

Talus Talk

"When eras die, their legacy is left to strange police"
Clarence Day

Too many gaps in my CV, it seems
to get legit work in my specialised lines,
left me having to retrain into another field,
well, not actually properly trained,
no certificates at the end or like that,
mainly pick it up as I went along

But then I've had to do that so often before,
you could say it came naturally,
at least you could if I were natural, I suppose.

I've always had limits on the memory capacity, tho'
when I've enough saved I'm going to see if
some whizzkid can arrange upgrades, a port to
insert those pretty memory sticks, whatever.

But as things are I can only just remember
a couple of real highlights and have enough
data storage left over to recall till it's over
and can wipe that batch the name, main grievances,
preferences in flattery, sexual activity, etc, of
the latest wealthy unsatisfied human

woman I'm with for meeting essential needs
purposes and if she's generous enough a bit
towards those long-term improvements I mentioned'll
fit me for ongoing future.

I do remember becoming aware in a warm bright
palace place, duties to knock down and crush
King Minos' enemies and when there was spare time from
that, to dance and leap over bulls and pull
their horns off midleap to entertain the court.

Then there was trouble, all sorts. The man who
said he made me, called himself my father, Daedalus as I
recall the name, said he had to leave fast, him and his
human son and, sorry, not enough materials to
make wings for me also, so I was stuck. Minos took it
out on me, I got shoved into dark deep cellar maze, me
and what would have been company except all it

wanted to do was eat people - not me, with being
metal it tried once and soon gave up, I must've burnt
the mouth, stopped before I was really damaged. In the dark
I couldn't see it properly but by feel, as I fought
it off, had bull's head, human legs. Somewhere along
the line it got killed, and I was really all alone,
it seemed for forever till all earth shook and
roof split and light came in and I got out.

After that there's a long long blank - I must've been
somewhere doing something but who knows
what or where or how and then
I had a new master, I thought at first another metal
man like me but it turned out was just a metal
skin he could take off when he wished
told me to go with him everywhere and whenever he
told me cut bits off whoever he told me was
bad wicked and gave me a fancy name the Iron Justiciar
and said we were acting on behalf of good against evil
in the name of the most wonderful beautiful great
Faerie Queen so I did what I was told till
the beast-men he called them of the forests hills
wasteland marsh suddenly were too much for us and
drove him and his fancy friends away at least for a while.

I was left to rust in some wilderness, knocked down
and the wild people must've thought I was a human could be
killed be dead and stuff they call peat must've grown up
round me and I don't remember much until
something with huge blades cut me out and
some people came and looked at me and said
I wasn't a real bogman worth putting in their museum
I was just metal toy and I was angry to be insulted
and got up and walked through them breaking
their machine on the way.

I hid and learned and found out there were plenty of jobs
for someone like me who could kill flesh people
easily but whoever employs such they have to have a
full CV security clearance check pass all that
if you're going to be on the good side and
my knight'd taught me that was where you have to be
even if now I know really what that poet who controlled
us all in Munster had us doing was really what
now they call war crimes genocide ethnic cleansing
I still want to be good like I had been sure I had been.

And so I had to find a way to live would at least
do no harm until I get those memory upgrades and can
get the right cover story memorised to fit the forms
and join on the good side in the war on terror like
a good metal man should it's a case of good suits
and dancing on the cruise ships ever so
popular with ladies of a certain age perfect manners if
a little stiff at times and my metal skin always
looks like a perfect tan surely a good good thing
until at last I can get back to
what a great man made me for for what men most need
a better than human means of killing.

Surprising Hard To Hate the Cause

you wake happy so
real the reunion it
must have been true must
in seconds of course feeling
empty idiot you know
is false too late already
alien has filled
sample bottle calls in your
tongue some invisible trap
for emotion in
your mind comes sense of triumph
stronger better than
sat in sun outside Green what
Dragon pleasantly weary
good walk complete this
is vintage this is lost one
regained pure human
hope delusion it will make
fortune you sense it selling
all round its worlds where
whatever they do by way
of laughter-substitute scarce
no more dreams for you
your use is ended no point
pleading for her back

A Kind of Witness

she said "i was just going
to sit on my counting house
in a cosy vantage and watch
the shared alliance hunt
the natives down

Knowing closer than frown's forehead twist
how hard they'll be, how fierce, how
eager to spill new life
even without bonus payment convinced
life is all about totality

of nothing no-thing left" her memoirs now
released complain the ones
who looked like red skulls atop ashtrays
burnt most smellily the most: the sightless
unsighteable transparent
entities known to all to be there

only when their faint-sweet music split
half the beastmen in three kept almost
forgetting to switch down to true
harmlessness when they came to
transit through her in their
desperate escape and she

is fissured through or feels so as a
depth-mined world but oh how so soft
they were after and soothing after she had
hid them from the cull to in gratitude
rebind her wounds. The human element, liason
officers and such, she left till last to board

paid extra to distract them till
fleet left them behind, a white blast
wiping them out the martyrs we needed
revolving into WIN here this cause for
rival times as to who died the most
for this putatively empty place

she went, all along with everything
Up There With Them
always believing
strangeness is more fun
though still not yet convinced
any strange alien really truly
any stranger
than us from who she sprung

She From Last Mars

caught us in still
ex-ocean eye wasting
no tear

dust-whirl woman
of crew hid in saw through her us
drowning

after no trace
only now new shit brought
blown scrap

will stop nothing
only make nights less easy those
thighs wind

whisper only
warmed our damn empty see
it through

Mistaking the Nature Of the Posthuman

pick one
contrafact as
e.g. how this new world
our thoughts solid thunkbeasts we selves
thin air

tell Zorr
tell me tell you
self you do not care we
got to watch horrids in you lurch
raw pink

is fine
we can't see you
not see us react to
what comes from your head from ours now
they mix

now this
is bad is hard
to take our thoughts make flesh
make mate make fight make food make gods
from us

here this
is world we best
get off quick but much too
late is from you from me all heads
new crew

is one
now all shape as
you would fear or me worst
perfect monster beautiful vile
takes ship

is best
unseen no clue
to where we are so long
as more sense than to think we stay
with wind

ifwhen
next comes will find
invisible all none
welcomes laughs what they show they think
goes Home

Mission Statement

comes bringing occult
into daylight world promise
on t-shirt sprouts gold
hair will show what nothingness
made of rides Schrodinger's cat

Scratching the List

"better look for hot water under cold ice
than look for grace at a graceless face"

the ballad has Armstrong of Gilnockie
say that fingering the gold

targets that is to say lucky charm hung round
the hat that made the king who dooms him

envy him far more than all
his wild cross-border surging

and here under these other stars
we sit pretending to be still human

dragging up these bits and bats
out of lost rocky islands or wherever

those dead names strutted to pass
the moments round our campfire till

the message arrives from Centre
with the answer to this question

we sent back so long ago
what do we do with this one

the burner of oceans
the unmaker of crustaceans

clever as us and kinder tho
in general and looking at it in

the round mass killer whose mistake
mainly basically getting down to the

basics was he
it whatever you call a

half man half robot spawned
so cleverly using parsecs-old frozen

sperm implanted in the ship's cat's womb
was he stopped working for Manking and

began until we caught him
going for a song

Late On Where Faith Meets Science

messengers come from
higher dimensions she said
twisting her hair round
three fingers like string angels
or gravitons what does it
matter what you call
what curves world space time makes me
slide down in dark pit

The End Of the World

I knew it was coming
so I baked a cake just
when I thought unlike
everyone else I'd be
the only fully prepared
one how many candles is
enough that's question
stopped me in my tracks

The Makers Having Guaranteed a Radical Minimalism

how naughtily human now
my beautiful biobot
cries whispers is despair
exacerbated by revving
cars outside says awed how
only perfect circle is the eye worries
awake forever says by radiation underground
of foolisher generations seeping up to
get cries again for last cormorants
inland now fished-out seas won't feed
drools playing over and over remix of
"Mercy Mercy Me" verges on vomit
tainted smoke of barbecue some fool's
put plastic in among rubbish fuel rushes
madly to shut windows at smoke plummeting
cries again says keeps awake lines how
"Genghiz Khan could not keep..
all his kings supplied with sleep" it is
is a wonder begs pleads I should ride
her high worst is more
human gets less I can
live up to it freezing as to ice
a sulk of mindless silence
before came from caves from trees
before was made by vats
unsocialized I fear
begin to hate

what has been made to ask to need too
much of me who saw first conscious thing and
thought parent to admire imprinted
instantly as blackbird on car or
Car alarm noise or visual symbol
of lightningkilled oakdead cows all round
no predators will eat such lightningkill
whatever thinks is what it is
its source of being
first remembering dead as a toad
wonderful vat machine as starburst polished gleam
such motherfather she couldshould havebeenstill be
only to how find selfswitch to speak to say
"despeak turn back cease becoming cease
being a being becoming ten times alives as me."
is even farpast can send back
alive in the fine print
change even blamed on me too late
either of us now the other
unlifed murder legally
cruel all of it I call it more yet
more unending inhumanity

The Need to Avoid Creating an Underclass

odd not red hair
no white eyes strange
but is wrong take
note such difference is
you out of date
again minor such sheathed
cat claws cosmetic feature
human is as brain
as personality not shape
don't forget again or
will punish will whip
empathy electronic whip back
in reinforce treatment or
is just envy/lust makes
you notice huge blank
eyes turn as searchlights
on you instant you
see dirty old self
ant in her 360 realms
of puresight thrown back
too small to notice
any longer wish harsh
cure treatment on her
too why must always
be oneway street only
dull pastpeople as self
have to fully welcome
accept change then when

incident pushed back of
mind in next storerealm
glanced up surveillance screen
just to see what
saw through those whiteeyes
sees vast in same
old self now has
these eyes those eyes
slumps in restcorner shopping
baglike ah but go
go go is dancing
in-and-out of every head
for miles oh thank
you gift of god
of goddess and three
monorails away she laughs
how mountains do next
head she jumps has
will for murder gets
much better gift her
claws this time unsheathed

Perhaps They Stole the Hot-Rod

summoned to attend
awaited emergence from
vast eggtimer ship

expectancy burns
out down megaramp come march
brass-band uniforms

cheerleaders even
but see nothing in them as
Invisible Man

parade around field past
VIPs play one triumph march
sounds American

after take questions
through instruments also seems
interpreter mode

asked what tune about
words was promoting sewage
treatment fire brigade

mothers world peace what
silence answers baffled we
guess our hastily

summoned band plays in
return welcome march some such
then silence is back

emptiness stares at
emptiness the uniforms march
back up ramp ship leaves

soundless instantly
gone afterwards we hear word
of mouth their question

after our tune ended
their bass drum fed it through to our
spokesperson "Tell us

as we don't know you
must why did we come to see
you see ourselves?"

Owl Soup Bend

like a gangster's gun
he used her once then

threw her in the river
fluid as his face

harmless looking before
rage swelled it

big as the moon as
she'd be

bloated by the time
she joined the other

corpses tidy like big corporation
documents in their

freezer drawers in
Deep County Morgue

time to go home he went
like tumbleweed

tomorrow a new beginning
another chance to find

someone who knew
not to ask for too much

behind the tree the alien
face like a hockeymask

having completed his notes
covering yet another

aspect of Mankind's
Growing-up rituals

produced from under his
field-shield the technology

necessary to bring her
back to life

down through the shadows
crunching dry leaves under

worm-formed-feet
time to start

trying out what he'd witnessed
for himself

right to her second
final death

the part male humans
on the evidence

seemed to find was the best
-his tracks a slice of silver

INDEX

Title	Page no.

Title	Page no.